S0-DVD-451

LIVING A LIFE
ACCORDING TO
THE HIGH PEAK OF
GOD'S REVELATION

Witness Lee

Living Stream Ministry
Anaheim, California • www.lsm.org

© 1994 Living Stream Ministry

All rights reserved. No part of this work may be reproduced or transmitted in any form or by any means—graphic, electronic, or mechanical, including photocopying, recording, or information storage and retrieval systems—without written permission from the publisher.

First Edition, July 1994.

ISBN 978-0-87083-791-3

Published by

Living Stream Ministry
2431 W. La Palma Ave., Anaheim, CA 92801 U.S.A.
P. O. Box 2121, Anaheim, CA 92814 U.S.A.

Printed in the United States of America

08   09   10   11   12   13   /   13   12   11   10   9   8   7

CONTENTS

PREFACE

The messages contained in this book were given by Brother Witness Lee in Anaheim, California on July 7-9, 1994, at the conclusion of the Summer Training on 1 and 2 Kings.

CHAPTER ONE

THE FULFILLMENT IN THE NEW TESTAMENT OF THE TYPOLOGY IN THE OLD TESTAMENT CONCERNING GOD'S ECONOMY

(1)

THE PICTURE AND THE DEFINITION OF GOD'S ECONOMY

We need to see the fulfillment in the New Testament of the typology in the Old Testament concerning God's economy. What is in the Old Testament is a typology, a set of types. Then what is in the New Testament is a complete fulfillment of that typology concerning God's economy. Thus, the entire Bible, both the Old Testament and the New Testament, is first a picture of God's economy and then a full definition and fulfillment of God's economy. On the one hand, if we want to know the Old Testament, we must come to the New Testament definition. In the Old Testament, we can see only the pictures. On the other hand, if we want to know the New Testament, we have to spend the time to look at all these pictures.

Saint Augustine said that the New Testament is concealed in the Old Testament, and the Old Testament is unveiled in the New Testament. So these two sections are on the same thing. In today's schools the good lesson books have pictures and then definitions. The pictures and the definitions form a strong basic principle for us to understand the Bible. If you do not know this principle, you will create mixture and confusion from the teachings of the Bible.

Two groups of Christians—those in the Catholic Church and those in Pentecostalism—are the top "experts," "specialists," in mixing up the Old Testament with the New Testament. In the Pentecostal movement, they sing a lot of Bible verses. All the verses they sing are from the Old Testament. Ephesians is a top book and Romans is a basic book in the New Testament, but they do not sing verses from these books. They sing mostly from the Psalms or from Isaiah. This is because the Pentecostal people do not know God's New Testament economy. They miss the New Testament definition. They like some of the Old Testament pictures without understanding them. In other words, they like to look at the pictures; they do not like to read the definitions. If you look at a picture without the proper definition, you may consider a lion as a tiger or a turtle as a mouse. The Pentecostals' expounding of the Bible is a mixture because they do not have the proper definitions. It is the same in principle with the practices of Catholicism. The clothing of the cardinals and archbishops is a mixture. Mostly their robes are made according to the style of the robes of the Aaronic priests in the Old Testament.

In the early years of my Christian life, I was with the Brethren. They were famous for understanding the Old Testament types and prophecies, and I received much knowledge from them. The great teachers among the Brethren said that the entire history of Israel was a type of the church. Without this understanding, we cannot explain the significance of the books of Ezra and Nehemiah. These books are a record of the return of the children of Israel from captivity. The teaching of the Brethren strongly stressed that the captivity of Israel into Babylon typifies the church which was captured into Catholicism. Even the Lord Jesus pointed this out. The Lord Jesus referred to the Roman Catholic Church as Jezebel (Rev. 2:20; Matt. 13:33) and also as the Great Babylon, a mystery (Rev. 17:5). The entire Catholic Church is a mystery in what she is, in what she practices, and in what she teaches. The Brethren saw that Israel's captivity typified the church's captivity and that the return of Israel typified the recovery of the church starting from Luther. There is a call in the book of Revelation to come out of Babylon, to come out of the Catholic Church (18:4).

Although the Brethren saw this, they did not see that the history of the kings in the Old Testament was a typology of God's economy. Actually, not one of the great teachers of the Brethren saw the economy of God. They did not even use this term. They somewhat used another term to replace *God's economy,* that is, *God's plan* or *God's purpose.* The English word *economy* is anglicized from the Greek word *oikonomia.* But who knows today what God's economy is? When most think of an economy, they think of it in terms of dollars and cents. We do not mean this when we speak of God's economy. God's economy is God's plan, God's divine arrangement, for the fulfillment of His good pleasure in His will to be His purpose. Israel's history was not only a type of the entire church, as the Brethren teachers pointed out, but also a type of God's economy. The fulfillment of this economy is in the New Testament. The New Testament presents us the complete fulfillment of the typology of the kings in the Old Testament. Thus, there is the typology in the Old Testament and the fulfillment in the New Testament. One is the picture, and the other is the definition.

THE NEED FOR THE OVERCOMERS

Eventually, both the Old and New Testaments end with the overcomers. In the age of typology, the overcomers were the prophets. The prophets took care of God's oracle first. Based upon their oracle, they did exercise, to some extent, God's authority. A number of kings listened to the prophets. Even Nathan was the authority over David. David was the king, and Nathan was the prophet. It was not Nathan who listened to David, but David to Nathan. In this sense, Nathan was God's authority. Thus, all of the genuine prophets were overcomers. Surely, Daniel and his three friends were overcomers.

This is fulfilled in Revelation, the last book of the New Testament. The Lord Jesus realized that the church was a great and complete failure. Just by the church in itself, there was no hope for the carrying out of God's economy. So in His seven epistles to the churches, He sounded the trumpet to call the overcomers. In that one book, in just two chapters, the

Lord repeated the following word seven times: *he who over-comes.* This is repeated at the end of each of the seven epistles (Rev. 2:7, 11, 17, 26; 3:5, 12, 21).

These overcomers are the fulfillment of the typology of the prophets. Therefore, when the apostle Paul was talking about how the church should meet, he stressed and uplifted prophesying (1 Cor. 14:1, 3-6, 24, 31, 39). Prophesying makes you an overcomer. Speaking Christ into people is prophesying. Prophesying is the function of the overcomers.

The overcomers in both the Old and New Testaments, in principle, are the same. Most of them were martyred. They sacrificed everything for the Lord. Paul was the leading one. He worked much for the Lord and wrote fourteen Epistles, but eventually he was martyred. Second Timothy tells us he knew that martyrdom would come to him, and he was ready to accept it (4:6-8). He was a man always living a life not by himself, but by Christ mingled with him. So he could say, "For to me, to live is Christ" (Phil. 1:21a). He was a person like Jesus, a person who was always crucified. He was a person crucified to live, or dying to live, denying the self, the natural man, and living, acting, and behaving all the time by the indwelling Christ who had been mingled with him.

Today the Lord has raised up the recovery after all the failures. The Lord tried with Israel. Israel failed. The Lord tried with the church. The church failed. So this forced the Lord to call out the overcomers. Eventually, seventy-two years ago, the Lord went to China to raise up the recovery there with Brother Watchman Nee, and the first messages he gave were concerning the overcomers. He expounded the entire book of Revelation. Brother Nee stressed the same thing as Jessie Penn-Lewis, who published a paper called *The Overcomer,* and he translated into Chinese the important books written by Mrs. Penn-Lewis on the overcoming life.

It was a difficult thing, however, for Brother Nee to put out his ministry. His ministry, to most Christians, was like the playing of music to cows. What cow can understand the music? I was there with him. I realized that even some of his co-workers were cows. They did not know what Brother Nee taught. Then I came to this country. I found out that there were a good number in this country who were not cows, who had been prepared by the Lord. This was why in the early days of my time in this country, my ministry was warmly welcomed by these prepared people. When they heard this ministry, they immediately turned to the recovery.

Gradually, however, we have become somewhat dull, losing the real sense of the Lord's recovery, not living a life under the cross by the power of resurrection, a life of denying the self and crucifying the flesh all the time by the resurrection of Christ. This is why I decided in 1984, after having been in the United States for over twenty years, to stop the work here and return to Taiwan to study our situation in order to bring us into the God-ordained way. Since 1984 I have published many messages on the New Testament economy of God. Many of us have read these messages, but I do not think that we really realize them. I believe that the Lord, because of this, has given me a further vision, a further revelation, to present as I am doing today. This further revelation began with the 1991 Thanksgiving conference in Reston, Virginia (*The Intrinsic View of the Body of Christ*) and continued with the following Thanksgiving conferences in Atlanta in 1992 (*The Constitution and the Building Up of the Body of Christ*) and in Anaheim in 1993 (*The Issue of the Dispensing of the Processed Trinity and the Transmitting of the Transcending Christ*). The messages in those three conferences are in principle the same as the messages I am giving today. The speaking of the ministry with the utterances and expressions is always improving, not by myself but by the Lord's further revelation. So my burden is very heavy, and the Lord covers me with His prevailing blood against the enemy. I am full. I need more conferences. But my physical body has been under the enemy's attack. Please pray for this.

We have to see the New Testament fulfillment of the top typology of God's eternal economy. We all must be Nazarites. We have to live a life like Jesus did on the earth, denying the self, rejecting the flesh, taking the cross, which means bearing the cross to be crucified every day. We need to be a person crucified to live by another Person, another life, which is the embodiment of the Triune God mingled with us. This

Person is the resurrection, and this resurrection is the power. When we live such a Person, we are today's fulfillment of the typology of God's economy.

We are today's fulfillment as we live a life that can reach the kingship. This is according to what Romans 5:17 says: "Much more those who receive the abundance of grace and of the gift of righteousness will reign in life." In all of our situations, we should reign as kings in life. Dear saints, we must live a Christian life which is the overcoming life, the life of an overcomer. All the overcomers of the New Testament are kings who have received the abundance of grace and of the gift of righteousness to reign in life. These four words—*grace, righteousness, reign, life*—are together in this one verse, verse 17 of Romans 5. God has given Himself to us as grace, and this grace has abundance. Going along with His grace, God has given us a gift, and this gift is God Himself as righteousness. God as grace for our enjoyment and God's righteousness are given as a gift to us. These two things will issue in a life to reign, a life to be kings. I hope that you could receive this word. Let God bless you to make you an overcomer today, living a life that is the life to reign.

THE FULFILLMENT IN THE NEW TESTAMENT OF THE TYPOLOGY IN THE OLD TESTAMENT CONCERNING GOD'S ECONOMY

(2)

In this chapter I want to continue to fellowship concerning the fulfillment in the New Testament of the typology in the Old Testament concerning God's economy. The whole Bible unveils God's economy, which is for the accomplishment of His heart's desire for His good pleasure. The center and the reality of God's economy is Christ and His Body.

ISRAEL BEING A TYPE OF THE CHURCH

Before the new testament age, that is, before the Lord's incarnation, God had chosen a people on this earth called Israel. This people of God's selection has a long history. Their forefather was Abraham. Then by Moses' time at their exodus from Egypt, they became a race that had at least two million people. Since then they have become a type of the church as God's elect in the New Testament. Thus, the Old Testament has a people, and the New Testament has a people. The Old Testament has Israel, and the New Testament has the church. These two peoples do not represent two things God has done. These two peoples are a description of one thing which God has done, and this one thing is the accomplishment of God's economy. Before God came to accomplish this economy, He first put out a type, a figure, a shadow. In God's economy the people of Israel are just a type, a figure, a shadow. They are not the real thing. Israel typifies the church.

I would like to present some verses from the New Testament to show that the people of Israel are a type of the church. In 1 Corinthians 5 Paul said, "Our Passover, Christ, also has been sacrificed" (v. 7b). After the descendants of Abraham became a people, they eventually became fallen into the hand of Egypt and its king, Pharaoh. Pharaoh typifies Satan, and Egypt typifies the world. This means that God's chosen people fell into the hand of Satan and Satan's world, so there was the need of God's salvation to save them.

God's salvation must first be judicial. God cannot come to save us nonsensically. Because God has to carry out His salvation judicially, there was a need of redemption for God's salvation. In Exodus we see two things. First, there is redemption, and then immediately following redemption, there is salvation. Redemption is to redeem God's fallen people back to God, and salvation is God's saving His people out of the hand of Satan, out of the world, and eventually, even out of themselves for God to come in to make them the same as God. So in Exodus we see that first a lamb was slain and the shed blood was sprinkled on the houses of Israel. That was called the Passover. This means that God, the just God, the righteous God, formed something judicial to redeem His people by fulfilling His righteous requirements. That was God's redemption.

Then immediately following that redemption, God exercised His salvation to save Israel out of Pharaoh's hand, out of Egypt, and bring them into the wilderness. In the wilderness God came to be a tabernacle, indicating how He would come to dwell with His people to save them further and further that they might become God in life and nature but not in the Godhead. This is God's salvation.

Paul said in 1 Corinthians 5 that our Passover is Christ. Christ became our Redeemer to accomplish a passover by which God could pass over us, having our sin judged and dealt with by Christ on the cross. First Corinthians 5 also says that following the Passover Israel had the Feast of Unleavened Bread (v. 8). After God's redemption and in God's salvation, God ordained that His people should have no sin, no leaven, a feast without leaven. This is the beginning of the history of Israel, and this beginning was fulfilled by the church's experience of Christ. By this you can see that with Israel it was a type. With the church it is a fulfillment.

At the end of the New Testament, the Lord Jesus called the degraded church, Jezebel (Rev. 2:20). Jezebel was an evil woman as a wife to that evil king, Ahab (1 Kings 16:31; 19:1-2; 21:23, 25-26; 2 Kings 9:7). She did many demonic things. She was a type of the church becoming degraded and fallen absolutely into Satan's hand and even mingled with Satan as one. The fallen church became Jezebel and is called the Great Babylon, the mystery (Rev. 17:5). Eventually, the outcome of the church is the same as that of Israel. Israel's outcome was to be captured to Babylon. Eventually, they became Babylon. In Revelation 17 the Lord called the degraded church the great whore, the Great Babylon, the mother of harlots (vv. 1, 5). This shows that the church is a fulfillment of the type of Israel. So the entire history of Israel is a type of the church.

THE TYPE OF THE KINGS, PRIESTS, AND PROPHETS

In the type of Israel, there is a great part concerning the kings. The kings are the representatives of Israel and the top ones. Israel was mainly enjoying the good land. They had everything of their living from the source of the good land. The top ones, who were enjoying the good land on the top level, were the kings. These kings are types of the New Testament believers, because all of the New Testament believers were saved by God to be kings. Every New Testament believer is to be a king and a priest (1 Pet. 2:9; Rev. 1:6; 5:10; 2 Tim. 2:12).

Both the kings and the priests are the deputy authority of God. The deputy authority of God is composed of God's oracle to speak and God's authority to rule. In the Old Testament, the first group ordained by God to speak for Him as His oracle was called the priests. Actually, God entrusted to the priests not only the speaking part of His deputy authority but also the ruling part. Thus, the priests were the speakers and also the kings. God, however, does not want a king to replace Him. He just wants His authority to be exercised. So at the beginning of Israel's history with the priests, there was no king, but they did have the Urim and the Thummim. The Urim and the Thummim were a deputy authority for both God's speaking and God's ruling (Exo. 28:30; Lev. 8:8). Because Israel adopted the custom of the nations, they wanted to have a king. Thus, God gave them a negative king named Saul. Actually, God Himself was their King already. Israel's real king was not a human person but God Himself.

In the New Testament, all the believers were saved to be kings and priests. When the priests speak for God, they become God's spokesmen, God's mouthpiece, and these are the prophets. So in the New Testament, we believers are kings, priests, and prophets. The kings of the Old Testament were a type, and this type is fulfilled by the New Testament believers being kings. These are the people who enjoy Christ to the uttermost.

Romans 5:17 says that "those who receive the abundance of grace and of the gift of righteousness will reign in life." John 1 says that when God came in His incarnation, grace came (vv. 14, 17). When God came to be a man, that was grace coming. Grace is the Triune God as our enjoyment. We all have received this grace in abundance. It is not just abundant grace but abounding grace, which is increasing all the time. We have received this grace, and we have received a gift from God, which is also abounding. This gift is God's righteousness for our redemption judicially. Thus, we have received these two things: grace and righteousness. These are for us to reign in life, to be kings in life.

If we have not reached the level of a king in our Christian life, we are still below the proper standard. We may say that we enjoy Christ, but to what degree, to what extent, do we enjoy Christ? Our enjoyment of Christ may be only "one inch high," but Christ is unlimited. Our enjoyment of Christ should come up to the kingship level. As the God-ordained prophets and priests, we are also kings to rule over all the enemies of God. God rules, but He does not rule directly. God rules through us, through the believers, as kings. The believers in the New Testament should be the fulfillment of the typology of the kings in God's economy.

Now we need to see how we can be such kings. We can be such kings only by being men regenerated with God and transformed with God as the element, so that we live not by our own life, by ourselves, by our natural man, or by our flesh. Instead, we live by God who is now mingling Himself with us as one. The believers' life is to live such a human yet divine life. It is in this life that we can be kings to enjoy our God-ordained portion, which is Christ as our good land.

Our fellowship here is not a man's teaching or some kind of theology discovered by Bible students. This is a revelation, just like the book of Revelation. The book of Revelation presents us a view, not teachings. My fellowship here is a revelation showing you a view. It is altogether not doctrines or facts in black and white as a record.

Now we need to consider where we should be according to this revelation. We all have to answer, "We should be in the resurrection." The resurrection of Christ eventually should become the place where we stay. We were God's created people who became fallen. Now we are God's redeemed people based upon His choosing of us, and we are also God's regenerated and transformed people who have been transformed with God's element to make us God-men. Now we are here in resurrection. To be in resurrection means to deny everything old to become something new and live by the element of newness, which is the divine life, God Himself.

In resurrection we have become God's new creation (2 Cor. 5:17; Gal. 6:15). This new creation is God's re-created, regenerated, transformed people. This is also the church in localities and the Body of Christ universally. Whether in the church locally or for the Body of Christ universally, we should be a person in resurrection.

Do not forget that when you open your mouth to speak Christ into people, you become God's oracle and God's prophet. Then you become a good priest. Samuel was such a person. He was not a priest according to God's ordination from the tribe of Levi. But he became a priest by prophesying for God, and this priest brought in the kingship. Thus, when you speak, you will be a prophet. Then your prophetic ministry will bring you into the kingship.

CHAPTER THREE

THE FULFILLMENT IN
THE NEW TESTAMENT OF
THE TYPOLOGY IN THE OLD TESTAMENT
CONCERNING GOD'S ECONOMY

(3)

Scripture Reading: Gal. 5:16, 24-25; Rom. 8:4-6; 1 Cor. 6:17; Rev. 1:4; 4:5; 5:6; 1:10a; 22:17a; John 7:37-39

In this fellowship my burden is to turn us all to the mingled spirit. Two spirits—the divine Spirit and the human spirit—are entwined and mingled as one.

THE REVELATION OF THE SPIRIT IN THE BIBLE

The Spirit in the Old Testament

Genesis 1:1 says that God created the heavens and the earth. Verse 2 then says that the Spirit of God was brooding over the death waters. Later, after man had fallen to such an extent that he had become flesh, Genesis 6:3 says that the Spirit of Jehovah would not strive with man any longer. Throughout the Old Testament the Spirit is referred to as either the Spirit of God or the Spirit of Jehovah. In Psalm 51:11 and Isaiah 63:10-11 the Spirit is referred to as the Spirit of God's holiness, but the divine title *the Holy Spirit* is not used in the Old Testament.

The Consummation of the Spirit
in the New Testament

At the beginning of the New Testament, when Christ was to be conceived and born, the Holy Spirit is mentioned for the first time (Matt. 1:18, 20). Christ's conception and Christ's birth were altogether by the Holy Spirit. Here the Holy Spirit is strongly stressed. Christ was conceived of this Spirit, and He was born through this Spirit.

While the Lord Jesus was walking on the earth and ministering for God, Matthew 12:28 tells us that He cast out demons by the Spirit of God. This indicates that the Spirit was with the Lord Jesus. However, John 7:37-39 says, "Now on the last day, the great day of the feast, Jesus stood and cried out, saying, If anyone thirsts, let him come to Me and drink. He who believes into Me, as the Scripture said, out of his innermost being shall flow rivers of living water. But this He said concerning the Spirit, whom those who believed into Him were about to receive; for the Spirit was not yet, because Jesus had not yet been glorified." Although the Spirit was with the Lord Jesus in His living and working on the earth, John 7:39 says that "the Spirit was not yet." The Lord lived on the earth for thirty years; then He ministered for three and a half years. He was born of the Spirit, and He worked through the Spirit of God. Then in John 7, near the end of His three-and-a-half-year ministry, He called the thirsty ones to come to Him and drink, and He said that they would have rivers of living water flowing out of their innermost being. The apostle John said that the Lord spoke here concerning the Spirit—not the Spirit of God nor the Holy Spirit, but *the* Spirit—whom the believers were about to receive; "for," John wrote, "the Spirit was not yet." The Spirit of God was there in Genesis 1, and the Holy Spirit was there in Matthew 1. Why, near the end of the Lord's ministry on this earth, did John tell us that the Spirit whom the believers were about to receive "was not yet"?

Before us, Andrew Murray saw that the Holy Spirit of God is something particular, yet *the* Spirit is something more. In his masterpiece *The Spirit of Christ,* in the chapter entitled "The Spirit of the Glorified Jesus," Andrew Murray wrote that "the Spirit of God as poured out at Pentecost was indeed something new." According to Andrew Murray, this Spirit, who is *the* Spirit in John 7:39, is something more than the Spirit of God, the Spirit of Jehovah, the Spirit of the holiness of God, and the Holy Spirit. Even with the Holy Spirit, the Spirit of God had not been consummated wholly; that is, He had not been completed in full. The Spirit was not consummated until the glorification of Christ. According to Luke 24:26 the glorification of Christ was His resurrection. When Christ entered into resurrection, He was glorified. His divine nature with the divine life in Him was released. Christ's glorification was like the blossoming of a flower. When a flower blossoms, it is glorified; all the contents of its life and nature are released and expressed. The contents of Jesus Christ are just God with His holy nature and holy life. Before His death and resurrection these contents were concealed in the shell of Christ's humanity. Once during the three and a half years of His ministry, on the Mount of Transfiguration, three of Christ's disciples saw Him transformed, or transfigured, before their eyes. All of a sudden His face shined like the sun, and His garments became as white as light (Matt. 17:2). That was His glorification, but it lasted only a short time. When He entered into resurrection, He was wholly glorified by releasing God with God's nature and God's life from within Him. Until that time *the* Spirit was not yet. It was at that time that *the* Spirit was produced. First Corinthians 15:45b tells us that "the last Adam [that is, Christ] became a life-giving Spirit." This life-giving Spirit is *the* Spirit, produced through and in Christ's resurrection.

By passing through all the processes—incarnation, human living, the all-inclusive death, and the all-releasing resurrection—the Triune God, the God in the Divine Trinity, was consummated as one Spirit, that is, the life-giving Spirit. This life-giving Spirit is the totality of the consummated Triune God. This is the clear revelation in the New Testament. First, God became a man. That man was Jesus Christ, who is the God-man in the flesh. He was God, but one day He put on man. Thus, He became both divine and human, having put the flesh upon Him. When He was crucified, He brought this man, that is, His humanity, to the cross and died there to terminate humanity. Then He resurrected to bring His humanity into divinity. Through this resurrection His humanity was made divine (Rom. 1:4), and He was born to be the firstborn Son of God (Acts 13:33; Rom. 8:29). Such a One, in His resurrection and with His resurrection, became the life-giving Spirit. This Spirit is the consummation of the Triune God. We all need to see this.

This is not my teaching. This is the divine revelation in the holy Word. Although the Nicene Creed, issued at the Council of Nicaea in A.D. 325, stresses the Divine Trinity and the person of Christ and also includes the Spirit, the Nicene Creed does not say anything concerning Christ as the last Adam becoming a life-giving Spirit. Therefore, the Nicene Creed is good but not complete. Many major denominations and the Catholic Church still accept this creed as their faith. However, they do not pay adequate attention to John 7:39 or 1 Corinthians 15:45. In my study of the Bible I read John 7:39 many times and wondered why this verse says that "the Spirit was not yet." I also considered very much the significance of the last Adam becoming a life-giving Spirit in 1 Corinthians 15:45. It was not until 1954, while I was working for the Lord in Taipei and Manila, that I received a full revelation of what I am now passing on to you. In that year in a summer training in Hong Kong I released this matter, telling the saints that today our Triune God is the consummated God, not the original God. The original God was merely divine; but after passing through incarnation, human living, death, and resurrection, this Triune God has been processed and consummated in the life-giving Spirit.

REGENERATION, SANCTIFICATION, RENEWING, TRANSFORMATION, AND CONFORMATION BY THE MINGLED SPIRIT

We were regenerated by this life-giving Spirit, not merely by the Spirit of God or the Holy Spirit. The Spirit of God was for God's creation, and the Holy Spirit was for Christ's conception. Now, the life-giving Spirit is for God's new creation (2 Cor. 5:17), for God's producing of many sons (1 John 3:2; Rom. 8:29), who are the believers. Our spiritual origin, that is, the origin of our being God's new creation, is the life-giving Spirit.

From the time of our regeneration this life-giving Spirit

remains in us and indwells our spirit (Rom. 8:16). First, He regenerated our spirit; then He remains in us by indwelling our regenerated spirit. Hence, these two spirits—the divine, life-giving Spirit and our spirit, which has been regenerated by the life-giving Spirit—are mingled together as one (1 Cor. 6:17). In the New Testament there are a number of verses indicating that these two spirits are one. In Paul's Epistles, especially in Romans and Galatians, when the Spirit is mentioned, it is difficult to discern whether the divine Spirit or the regenerated human spirit is referred to. Romans 8:4 says that God's righteousness is with those who walk according to the spirit. It is difficult to discern whether the word *spirit* in this verse refers to the Spirit of God or to our spirit. In his New Translation, J. N. Darby, a great teacher among the Brethren, also noted this difficulty. This is because *spirit* in verses like Romans 8:4-6 denotes the two spirits, God's Spirit indwelling our spirit as one spirit. In 1 Corinthians 6:17 Paul said, "But he who is joined to the Lord is one spirit," indicating that we are one spirit with the Lord. In Romans 8 Paul also said that we must set our mind on this mingled spirit. In verse 6 he said that the mind set on the mingled spirit is life and peace, but the mind set on the flesh is death. Thus, today there are two possibilities in our Christian life. The first is to set our mind, which represents our natural, soulish man, on the mingled spirit. Such a mind set on the mingled spirit becomes life and peace. The second possibility is to set our mind on the flesh, which issues in death.

The New Testament tells us that our being regenerated, sanctified dispositionally, renewed, transformed, and conformed to Christ's image are all accomplished through the life-giving Spirit in our spirit (John 3:6; Rom. 15:16; 1 Cor. 6:11; Titus 3:5; 2 Cor. 3:18; Rom. 8:2, 29). Apart from the mingled spirit, there is no regeneration, no sanctification, no renewing, no transformation, and no conformation. Thus, all our spiritual experience is by the two spirits mingled together as one.

As believers in Christ who are seeking Him, we all must learn to remain in this spirit. We must set our entire being on this mingled spirit and do things according to this spirit. We must have our being altogether in this spirit. This is my burden in this chapter. There are many books written to tell Christians how to do things, such as how to be holy and how to be victorious. However, not one of these how-tos is prevailing. Only one way prevails, that is, to set our entire being on the mingled spirit. If we will do this, life and peace will be ours, and we will walk, have our being, and do things continually, not only every day but even every moment, in and according to this mingled spirit.

THE CONSUMMATED SPIRIT
INTENSIFIED SEVENFOLD FOR
THE DEGRADATION OF THE CHURCH

Even with such an all-inclusive Spirit, the church still became degraded. This forced God to intensify this life-giving Spirit sevenfold. This sevenfold intensifying of the Spirit is referred to in Revelation as the seven Spirits of God (1:4; 4:5; 5:6). Actually, these are not seven different Spirits of God. The Spirit of God is uniquely one, but to meet the need of the degraded church, this Spirit has been intensified sevenfold. Thus, Revelation 1:4 says that the book of Revelation was written from the seven Spirits to the seven churches. Since the seven churches were degraded churches (Rev. 2—3), they needed the sevenfold intensified Spirit.

In Revelation 1:10 the apostle John told us that he was in spirit—the mingled spirit—on the Lord's Day. This means that John was a person who continually lived and walked in the mingled spirit. Then, at the end of Revelation, as a closing of the entire Bible, the Spirit and the bride speak together (22:17). The bride is the church (2 Cor. 11:2; Eph. 5:31-32), and the Spirit is the Triune God consummated to be *the* Spirit. This Spirit is the Husband to the church. This indicates that the consummated Triune God will marry the transformed tripartite church. Thus, these two will become a couple—the Triune God consummated to be the Husband, and the tripartite man transformed to be the bride. The issue of such a union is the New Jerusalem. In the New Jerusalem we can see the bride and also the consummated Triune God, that is, Christ as the Lamb (21:2, 9).

LEARNING TO LIVE, WALK, AND HAVE OUR ENTIRE BEING IN AND ACCORDING TO THE MINGLED SPIRIT

Dear brothers and sisters, I urge you to forget everything. Do not listen to all the distracting things. We simply need to take care of one thing. We need to realize that God has been consummated to be the life-giving Spirit, and now this Spirit, after regenerating us, indwells our spirit to be one with our spirit, to sanctify us, to renew us, to transform us, to conform us, and to seal us (Eph. 1:13; 4:30; 2 Cor. 1:22). Sealing means saturating, and saturating means dispensing. The Spirit seals us with His divine element by dispensing the entire God into our being. The issue of this is the church, the Body of Christ. Ephesians 4:4-6 says that there is one Body, one Spirit, one Lord, and one God and Father. These four constituted together are the Body of Christ, and this Body of Christ will consummate in the New Jerusalem. Today we must realize this. Then we will forget everything and simply walk, live, and have our being in and according to the mingled spirit. This is all that we need. When we live in this way, spontaneously we put our natural man, our old man, on the cross (Rom. 6:6). The cross brings in resurrection, which is not merely a thing but a living person, who is the consummated Triune God as the life-giving Spirit.

I hope that this fellowship will impress you to the extent that you will never forget it. I hope that you will not be able to erase this message from your being. Now you should be clear that to be a believer in Christ is simply to have your being in and according to the mingled spirit. In your family life, in your daily life, in your church life, and in your social life, you should live by this mingled spirit. When you live such a life, spontaneously you are crucified all the day. Actually, you are crucified to live. Crucifixion always leads you to live in resurrection, and this resurrection is just the processed Triune God as the life-giving Spirit.

CHAPTER FOUR

THE WAY TO WALK, LIVE, AND HAVE OUR BEING IN AND ACCORDING TO THE MINGLED SPIRIT

Scripture Reading: 1 Thes. 5:16-20; Rom. 10:12; Eph. 6:17-18; 2 Tim. 2:22

In this chapter I want to share the real burden on my heart for my concern about the Lord's recovery. The Lord has shown us His economy, and He has shown us the contents of His economy, especially throughout the past thirty-two years. Most of the messages from this ministry have been put on audio and video tapes and have also been printed in books, yet according to our observation, generally speaking, we do not practice what we have seen of the Lord. Therefore, in this chapter I will come from the high peak of God's revelation down to the place where our feet are, where we are. I hope that I can do my best to show you what our need is today. The fellowship in this chapter and the following chapter is also my burden, the real word on my heart, for the elders in the Lord's recovery.

THE PRACTICES NEEDED TO CARRY OUT GOD'S ECONOMY ACCORDING TO THE HIGH PEAK OF GOD'S REVELATION

Let us read 1 Thessalonians 5:16-20: "Always rejoice, unceasingly pray, in everything give thanks; for this is the will of God in Christ Jesus for you. Do not quench the Spirit; do not despise prophecies." In this portion of the Word, I ask you to pay attention to three points. First, pray unceasingly. Second, do not quench the Spirit. Third, do not despise prophecies.

Romans 10:12 says, "For there is no distinction between

Jew and Greek, for the same Lord is Lord of all and rich to all who call upon Him." Here it says that the Lord is rich. His riches are unsearchable (Eph. 3:8), but how can we participate in and enjoy the Lord's riches? Here is a very simple way. This way is to call upon Him.

Ephesians 6:17-18 says, "And receive the helmet of salvation and the sword of the Spirit, which Spirit is the word of God, by means of all prayer and petition, praying at every time in spirit and watching unto this in all perseverance and petition concerning all the saints." We teach the practice of pray-reading the Word based upon what Paul said here. Ephesians 6:17 says that the Spirit is the word of God. The Lord Jesus said, "The words which I have spoken to you are spirit" (John 6:63). The word in Ephesians 6:17 is not the word in black and white. This word equals the Spirit. The next verse, verse 18, tells us that we have to pray this word, and we have to be watchful concerning this kind of prayer. In other words, we have to be watchful concerning our pray-reading. This is not just to be watchful concerning our reading of the Bible or our prayer in a common way. This is a particular prayer of praying the word, making the word our prayer. In this sense, we do not need to compose a prayer, because our prayer is the living word of God.

Second Timothy 2:22 says, "But flee youthful lusts, and pursue righteousness, faith, love, peace with those who call on the Lord out of a pure heart." This verse charges us to pursue righteousness, faith, love, and peace. These items are the Lord Jesus Himself, so to pursue these things means to pursue Christ. Paul here itemized the practical points concerning Christ. Christ is our righteousness. Christ is our faith. Christ is our love. Christ is our peace. Our practice of living the life of a God-man is a constitution of Christ as righteousness, faith, love, and peace. Paul charged Timothy to pursue Christ as these items by calling on the name of the Lord. This calling is not just by yourself but with those who call on the Lord out of a pure heart.

You may think that we cannot see anything high in all these verses and that these things are common among us. My fellowship, which is my burden, is this. Yes, all these things have been gradually unveiled to us by the Lord in the past years, and they have even been printed in books. But in our practice, there is a big shortage. How much have you called on the Lord today? Do you pray-read the word consistently and adequately? Do you pray unceasingly? Do you fan the Spirit into flame (2 Tim. 1:6)? We are told not to quench the Spirit, but nearly all of us quench the Spirit every day.

Now in our church practice, we promote the matter of prophesying. But even thus far, not many churches are practicing this prophesying. Most of the saints who do practice prophesying do not realize what it means to prophesy in the church meetings. Some give a word of their kind of experience or feeling, or they tell a story in the meeting. That is not prophesying. To prophesy is to speak God's word to people. In this speaking, Christ is spoken forth by you. To prophesy is to speak Christ forth into people. This mainly means to minister Christ. We minister Christ to others by our speaking. You may excuse yourself by saying that you do not have the gift to speak as some brothers have. But can you say that you do not have the gift to speak for the Lord, to speak forth the Lord, and to speak the Lord into people? We all have this gift, a gift to speak Christ (1 Cor. 14:31).

To carry out God's economy according to the high peak of God's revelation, we need all these practices. We were charged to walk, to live, and to have our being in and according to the mingled spirit (Rom. 8:4). How can we do this? We can do this only by these few steps: calling on the name of the Lord, pray-reading His word as the Spirit, praying unceasingly, not quenching the Spirit, and not despising or ignoring prophesying. If you cut yourself off from these things, you are finished; you can never live the life of a God-man. A God-man's life is a life of calling on the Lord, pray-reading His word as the Spirit, praying unceasingly, not quenching but fanning the Spirit into flame, and not despising but respecting prophesying. If you miss any part of these few things, you miss a lot.

THE NEED FOR A GENUINE REVIVAL
AND A CORPORATE MODEL

I recently fellowshipped with the co-workers and elders by speaking a very frank word to them. I said, "Brothers, many of you still work for the Lord by doing affairs. Your kind of taking the lead among the saints is not according to the spirit, but according to your kind of realization. So you made a number of formalities, asking others to perform your formalities. This often causes opinions and even divisions." All the co-workers and elders from today onward should have a change. You have not been called by the Lord as a co-worker or an elder to carry out formalities. You have been called and assigned by the Lord to carry out God's economy, and God's economy is altogether centered on Christ, taking Christ as its reality. Without Christ, there is no economy of God. We may be very busy every day in the Lord's recovery in the church, and we may be very diligent and faithful, yet we do things which are not the contents, the reality, and the center of God's economy. So we need a turn.

I pray to the Lord, "Lord, grant us in Your recovery to have a genuine, real revival." We do not want a revival, however, like the many revivals which went on in the past. One famous revival took place in Wales from 1904 to 1906 under the leadership of Evan Roberts, who was a coal miner. In a short time, this revival became so prevailing that when people would go to Wales to preach the gospel, no one would be saved. This is because nearly everybody in Wales had been saved. When I came into the work of the recovery in 1932, only about twenty-six years later, I heard about that revival. By then it had become not as prevailing as it should have been. The issue of that revival in Wales did not last long.

Evan Roberts stressed spiritual warfare, how to fight against Satan. But today what we have seen of the Lord is not in that category. What we have seen of the Lord is in God's central lane, the economy of God, with Christ as its centrality and universality, with Christ as its center, reality, and everything. This Christ is now the life-giving Spirit indwelling our regenerated spirit to be one with our spirit (1 Cor. 15:45b; 1 Cor. 6:17).

For such a revelation which is so high, deep, and profound, the Lord needs a model. He needs a corporate people to be raised up by His grace through this high peak of the divine revelation to live a life according to this revelation. Then they will be the model. Even for pray-reading, we did not set up a strong and proper model. Where is the model of living a crucified life that we may live Christ? Even among us, this is not too prevailing. Where is the model of living Christ and magnifying Christ by the bountiful supply of the Spirit of Jesus Christ? Where is this life? We have these revelations released as messages printed in books, but where is the model?

My burden is that my fellowship could affect you to be burdened with me for the same thing. We have the local churches, but no model. For all the things the Lord has shown us, there is no model. With calling on the name of the Lord, there is no model. With praying unceasingly, there is no model. The Lord is rich unto all who call on Him, but there is no model of this. We are not that rich in the Lord's recovery because we do not have the genuine, living practice of calling on the Lord. If we have this model, we will be enriched by the Lord through our calling on Him.

Paul even tells us that we should pursue Christ not only by our own individual calling but also by our corporate calling with others who call on the Lord from their sincere and pure heart. This indicates that we do not only need to call on the Lord and pray-read the word of the Lord as the Spirit individually. We also need this corporately. In all the churches there should be groups of ten or fifteen saints who come together often to call on the Lord.

Calling on the Lord implies a lot. When you open your mouth with the exercise of your spirit to call on the Lord, right away you are under His shining. You are enlightened and exposed. Then you see all your defects, shortcomings, and mistakes. As a wife, you see your mistakes in dealing with your husband. As a husband, you see that the way you deal with your wife is altogether not in the spirit. Then you make a thorough confession of your sins, failures, mistakes, defects, trespasses, transgressions, and wrongdoings.

You cannot make such a thorough confession unless you are enlightened in the light of the Lord. Who can be enlightened in the light of the Lord? Only those who call on Him from a sincere and pure heart. This is the initial experience of Christ in calling on His name. Then the Lord will continue to transfuse all His particular riches into your spirit and even into your mind. In this way you will participate in and enjoy the Lord's riches.

All the messages I have passed on to you came to me in this way. If you do not touch the Lord, how can you see His light and receive His revelation? Do not think that all these revelations have come to us just because we studied the Bible thoroughly. I know some who have studied the Bible very diligently, but they only know the Bible according to the letter. In my home town, about sixty years ago, there was a brother who was a Chinese scholar in the Ch'ing dynasty. He was put into prison by the Ch'ing dynasty, and it was there that he got saved. After he was released from prison, he studied the Bible. Eventually he remembered every verse of the Bible, so we called him "the living concordance." If you wanted to know a verse of the Bible, you could ask him instead of going to the concordance. I knew him. But I can testify before the Lord that this brother who was a living concordance did not have much light. He could not tell you the truth concerning regeneration or the church. If you know the black and white, this does not mean that you know the Bible. The Bible is not just the black and white. The black and white is a conveyer to convey the spiritual, divine, intrinsic reality to us.

Paul in Ephesians 6 said that the Spirit today is the word. The Bible must become the word as the Spirit. This means your Bible must be one with the Spirit. Your Bible is the Spirit, and the Spirit is your Bible. How can we get this? There is no other way except by calling on the Lord, by touching the Lord daily and moment by moment. If we are all such persons living in the presence of the Lord by calling on Him, by praying to Him unceasingly day after day and hour after hour, we will be the reality of the fulfillment of the typology in 1 and 2 Kings.

This is my strong burden I would fellowship with the elders. Every local church needs this. Do not invent many formalities. You yourself should practice calling on the Lord. You yourself should practice pray-reading the word as the Spirit. You need to practice the unceasing prayer. You need to practice never quenching the Spirit, but rather, fanning the Spirit all the time into flame. You need to practice not despising any prophesying. You elders should take the lead to practice this. First, you be the model. Then your practice in such an intimate way with the Lord will influence the saints in your church. Especially as elders, you can exercise much influence over the members of the church.

Probably after about one year, your church will become a model. When we talk to people about the vision we have seen, they will say, "Where is such a church?" Then we can say, "I'll bring you to one so you can see the model." This is what we need now. I do not believe that we need further revelations. We have seen enough. The urgent need today is the practice of a kind of living that belongs to God-men, and the God-men are the very components of God's economy.

All the elders and co-workers should pursue this reality so that they will be made into a model by the Lord, a model living in the economy of God. Then they and their churches will become such a model. In my prayer, this is what I call the genuine revival. There are over two hundred churches in the United States. Just in Southern California alone, there are fifty churches. If all these churches would be such a model, that would be a prevailing testimony.

CHAPTER FIVE

A NEW REVIVAL BY LIVING
THE LIFE OF A GOD-MAN

My burden in this chapter concerns a new revival. We need a new revival, a revival that has never occurred in history. In the history of the church there have been a number of revivals. The Reformation at the time of Martin Luther can be considered a revival. However, that revival was a mixture. After the Reformation a number of small revivals took place. Out of these revivals the private churches, such as the Baptist church, the Presbyterian church, and the Methodist church, were produced. In the eighteenth century a great revival was brought in by Count Zinzendorf with the Moravian Brothers. This revival included the practice of the proper church life to some extent. A century later the Brethren were raised up in Great Britain. The revival that they brought in was improved and greater than that under Zinzendorf. Watchman Nee considered the Brethren revival as a fulfillment of the church in Philadelphia in Revelation 3, and D. M. Panton, a student of Robert Govett, said that the influence of the Brethren revival was greater than that of Luther's reformation. The difference was that Luther's reformation was widely propagated, but the Brethren revival was the opposite. Not wanting to make a show, the Brethren preferred to conceal themselves. Among them were a number of great teachers, including John Nelson Darby and William Kelly. Today it is difficult to find a photograph of one of the Brethren teachers. The Brethren revival was nearly like the sun shining at noon, but it lasted only a relatively short time. The most prevailing time of the Brethren revival was around 1850. By the end of the First World War the Brethren were divided into more than a thousand divisions. At that time the sun had set on the Brethren revival. At the beginning of the twentieth century the Welsh revival took place, which was quite prevailing but only for a short time.

Then the Lord went to China. As Brother Nee said, to the Lord's move China was a virgin land not touched fully by the deformed Christianity. Brother Nee told me privately that the Lord was forced to go from Europe and America to China to take a virgin land to begin something new from the third decade of the present century. From China the Lord's recovery has spread throughout the globe now, and it is here with us today. What kind of revival is this? A revival is always the practice, the practicality, of the vision that people have seen. Martin Luther saw a vision concerning justification by faith, and he began to practice what he saw. The Reformation came out of that practice. Zinzendorf saw something of the oneness of the church, and he practiced what he saw. At his time a number of groups of believers were suffering persecution by the Catholic Church and the state churches in northern Europe. Many of these persecuted believers fled to Zinzendorf's estate in Saxony in southern Germany, and Zinzendorf received them. After they arrived, they argued among themselves over their doctrinal differences. One Lord's Day Zinzendorf called them together and convinced them to stop their arguments. They signed an agreement to keep the oneness among them and to lay aside their differences in doctrine and in their religious backgrounds. On that day, history tells us, while partaking of the Lord's table, they experienced the outpouring of the Spirit. By this they all were revived. That should be considered as a kind of revival of the church life.

THE NEED OF A REVIVAL
IN THE LORD'S RECOVERY TODAY

What kind of revival do we have today? In other words, what kind of model has been raised up among us? As a rule a revival should always be the practice of the vision we have seen. However, from the time I came into the recovery I have been watching over the situation. From Brother Nee's time until today, for seventy-two years, our practice has never come up to the standard of our vision that we have received of the Lord. Brother Nee stressed two things: Christ as life to produce the church and the church as the Body of Christ to express Christ. But, sorry to say, it was not only the outsiders who did not know these things; even among Brother Nee's co-workers, who were my contemporaries, very few have fully entered into the realization of these two matters. Not to mention the matter of the Body of Christ, they did not even see the matter of Christ as life to us. They stressed matters such as leaving the denominations, baptism by immersion, head covering, and the way to practice the Lord's table. In 1934 a letter came to me from Brother Nee saying that our emphasis was not on leaving the denominations, on baptism by immersion, on head covering, or on the practice of the Lord's table. He added that from that day forward, whoever preached and taught only those four things was not our co-worker. He said that the vision we had received from the Lord concerned Christ as our life to produce the church, not as an organization but as a Body, an organism, to express Christ. This, he said, is what we have seen, and this is what we should preach and teach. Brother Nee wrote these words twelve years after the beginning of the recovery in China in 1922.

From the time that I began my ministry until today I have put out many books concerning the vision that we have seen. Through all the years, in mainland China, in Taiwan, in southeast Asia, and in the West today, in our practice we have never come up to the standard of what we have seen.

THE HIGH PEAK OF THE DIVINE REVELATION

In the past ten years the Lord has shown us His economy. According to my study of church history and the biographies of many saints, I would say that before 1984 God's eternal economy as the very reality and the center of the Bible was never seen by God's people so fully as today among us. To my knowledge, no other book has pointed out that God's eternal economy has Christ as its center and reality, with His Body, the organic Body of Christ, as the organism to the Triune God.

Today we have come to this high peak of God's divine revelation. I would even say that we have probably reached the highest peak of the divine revelation in the entire Bible. This is the divine revelation discovered by the believers through the past twenty centuries. According to my knowledge, the first divine revelation discovered by the church fathers was the revelation of the Triune God. In the first part of the Bible, the Old Testament held by the Jews, it is difficult to find out anything concerning the Triune God. The Old Testament uses the divine titles *Elohim* (Gen. 1:1, 26), *Jehovah* (Gen. 2:4; Exo. 3:13-15), and *Adonai* (Gen. 15:2; Exo. 4:10) in referring to God. The Old Testament also mentions the Spirit of God (Gen. 1:2). Then in the New Testament there is One by the name of Jesus Christ (Matt. 1:1). Who is this One? Is He Jehovah? Is He God? If we say that Jesus Christ is God, the Jews will consider this blasphemy (John 10:33). How could a Nazarene be God? We may say that Jesus Christ is the Son of God. However, in the Old Testament we cannot find the divine title *the Son of God*. Although 2 Samuel 7:14 does say that God has a son, referring to Christ, the Jewish rabbis do not understand this word.

After the New Testament was written, the first group of Bible students after the apostles were the church fathers. They discovered that in the Bible there is such a thing as the Triune God, because in Matthew 28:19 the Lord Jesus told His disciples, "Go therefore and disciple all the nations, baptizing them into the name of the Father and of the Son and of the Holy Spirit." The Lord Jesus did not tell His disciples to baptize people into the name of Elohim, or Jehovah, or Adonai, but into the name of the Father and of the Son and of the Holy Spirit. Before that time the Lord could not speak such a word, because before His resurrection the Spirit was not yet (John 7:39), that is, the Spirit was not yet consummated. The Lord spoke the word in Matthew 28:19 after His resurrection, while He stayed with His disciples for forty days prior to His ascension. Before the Lord's resurrection, not only was the Spirit not yet, but even the firstborn Son of God was not yet (Acts 13:33; Rom. 8:29). Before His resurrection the Lord Jesus was the only begotten Son (John

1:18; 3:16). Even this the Jews did not know. They had Isaiah
7:14 and 9:6 and no doubt had read these verses again and
again, but none of the Jews understood them. Isaiah 7:14
says, "Behold, the virgin will conceive and will bear a son, and
she will call his name Immanuel," and 9:6 says, "...a son is
given to us;...and His name will be called...Mighty God, Eternal Father." In Isaiah 9:6 both the Son and the Father are
mentioned, but the Jews could not understand this. They
could not put the pieces of the puzzle together. When the
church fathers read all these things in the Scriptures, they
considered them and eventually invented a word in Latin:
triune. Tri means "three" and *une* means "one." The phrase
the Triune God means "the Three-one God." God is the unique
God (1 Cor. 8:4, 6; Rom. 3:30; 1 Tim. 2:5; Deut. 4:35, 39); thus,
He is one. Yet He is the Father, the Son, and the Spirit; therefore, He is three. Hence, God is three-one, triune. The church
fathers discovered this fact.

Centuries later Martin Luther made a further discovery.
Luther saw the matter of justification by faith (Rom. 3:28).
He discovered that salvation is not by works but by faith.
After this, many other students of the Bible made further dis-
coveries. However, before us, no one ever discovered God's
economy with Christ as its centrality and universality and all
its reality. It was not until the last ten years that we put all
these things together to have a full picture of God's economy.
This is the highest peak of the divine revelation.

LIVING THE LIFE OF A GOD-MAN ACCORDING TO
THE HIGH PEAK OF THE DIVINE REVELATION

Since we have seen such a high peak of the divine revelation, we need to put into practice what we have seen. Our
practice will have a success, and that success will be a new
revival—the highest revival, and probably the last revival
before the Lord's coming back. As I said in the previous
chapter, we need a model. I do not mean that only some individuals should become a model. I mean that we need a
corporate model, a Body, a people who live the life of
a God-man. From today our practice should be to live the life
of a God-man by realizing the power of the resurrection of

Christ to take His cross as He did, to be crucified, to be conformed to His death, every day to live another One's life (Phil. 3:10; 1:21; Gal. 2:20). Our life, our self, our flesh, our natural man, and our everything were already brought to the cross by Him. Now we are living Him, so we should remain in His crucifixion to be conformed to the mold of His death every moment in every part of our life. That will cause us to spontaneously live Him as the resurrection (John 11:25). This is the living of a God-man.

This should be and this must be our church practice from today onward. If not, we are practicing something in vain. Our practice is not merely to have a church life in which everything is according to the Bible, a church life in which we baptize people by immersion, forsake the denominations, practice head covering, and have the Lord's table, absolutely according to the Bible. Some have come into the recovery because of these practices. They appreciate our family life, the church meetings, and the way we train our young people. However, these things should not be the goal of our practice. The goal of our practice should be to live the life of a God-man. This is the goal we should reach.

Our practice is not to live the life of any kind of natural man, good or bad. Our practice is to live the life of a God-man. A God-man is a man who is regenerated and transformed to be one with God, taking God as his life, his person, and his everything. Eventually, this one becomes God in His life and His nature, but not in His Godhead. This is a God-man. In the recovery today we should practice to live the life of such a God-man. This life is a life of crucifixion by and in and with resurrection. It is a life in which I have been crucified with Christ, and it is no longer I who live but He who lives in me (Gal. 2:20). Yet when He lives in me, He lives with me, with the result that I live with Him (John 14:19). He lives with me, and I live with Him. We two live together in the way of mingling, a mingling of God and man.

The highest family life, marriage life, and social life come out of such a life. This life is the life of the church and the life of the Body of Christ. Such a life is the reality of the Body of Christ. Such a life, like that of Jesus Christ in His thirty-three and a half years on the earth, saves us from all negative things, from small things and big things. In our marriage life it saves us from separation and divorce. In the church it saves us from opinion, division, despising, criticizing, and murmuring. In this life there is no criticism, no despising, no partiality, no division, no dissension, no opinion. In such a life we live the life of a God-man. With Him everything is new, everything is heavenly, and everything is divine, divinity mingled with humanity.

Wherever there is division, there is spiritual fornication, idolatry, self-glorification, and self-exaltation. Without self-exaltation, there could be no division. Living the life of a God-man saves us from all these negative things. To live such a life is to live Christ (Phil. 1:21), the very model of the God-man life.

Dear saints, this is my burden. We all need to live such a life—the older ones and the young ones, the brothers and the sisters, the elders and the common saints. If we do, we are faithful to what we have heard. Then the Lord will have not a model only by individuals but a model by a group of us. This is the model that the Lord needs to show to today's Christianity, a model of what His church should be.

If we live such a life, surely we will go out to contact people for the preaching of the gospel. A vital group is a group of this kind of people. The vital groups should not be practiced as a formality; they should be groups of people who live such a life. Our living the life of a God-man will save people, edify others, and build up the local churches even to the building up of the Body of Christ.

If we practice what we have heard, spontaneously a model will be built up. This model will be the greatest revival in the history of the church. I believe that this revival will bring the Lord back.

In conclusion, I would encourage you to try faithfully to practice living a God-man's life by contacting Him through calling on His name, pray-reading His living word, praying unceasingly, not quenching the Spirit, and not despising prophesying. May the Lord bless us with Himself as the life-giving Spirit that we may touch Him in the mingled spirit by these life practices.

ABOUT THE AUTHOR

Witness Lee was born in 1905 in northern China and raised in a Christian family. At age 19 he was fully captured for Christ and immediately consecrated himself to preach the gospel for the rest of his life. Early in his service, he met Watchman Nee, a renowned preacher, teacher, and writer. Witness Lee labored together with Watchman Nee under his direction. In 1934 Watchman Nee entrusted Witness Lee with the responsibility for his publication operation, called the Shanghai Gospel Bookroom.

Prior to the Communist takeover in 1949, Witness Lee was sent by Watchman Nee and his other co-workers to Taiwan to ensure that the things delivered to them by the Lord would not be lost. Watchman Nee instructed Witness Lee to continue the former's publishing operation abroad as the Taiwan Gospel Bookroom, which has been publicly recognized as the publisher of Watchman Nee's works outside China. Witness Lee's work in Taiwan manifested the Lord's abundant blessing. From a mere 350 believers, newly fled from the mainland, the churches in Taiwan grew to 20,000 in five years.

In 1962 Witness Lee felt led of the Lord to come to the United States, settling in California. During his 35 years of service in the U.S., he ministered in weekly meetings and weekend conferences, delivering several thousand spoken messages. Much of his speaking has since been published as over 400 titles. Many of these have been translated into over fourteen languages. He gave his last public conference in February 1997 at the age of 91.

He leaves behind a prolific presentation of the truth in the Bible. His major work, *Life-study of the Bible,* comprises over 25,000 pages of commentary on every book of the Bible from the perspective of the believers' enjoyment and experience of God's divine life in Christ through the Holy Spirit. Witness Lee was the chief editor of a new translation of the New Testament into Chinese called the Recovery Version and directed the translation of the same into English. The Recovery Version also appears in a number of other languages. He provided an extensive body of footnotes, outlines, and spiritual cross references. A radio broadcast of his messages can be heard on Christian radio stations in the United States. In 1965 Witness Lee founded Living Stream Ministry, a non-profit corporation, located in Anaheim, California, which officially presents his and Watchman Nee's ministry.

Witness Lee's ministry emphasizes the experience of Christ as life and the practical oneness of the believers as the Body of Christ. Stressing the importance of attending to both these matters, he led the churches under his care to grow in Christian life and function. He was unbending in his conviction that God's goal is not narrow sectarianism but the Body of Christ. In time, believers began to meet simply as the church in their localities in response to this conviction. In recent years a number of new churches have been raised up in Russia and in many eastern European countries.

OTHER BOOKS PUBLISHED BY
Living Stream Ministry

Titles by Witness Lee:

Abraham—Called by God	978-0-7363-0359-0
The Experience of Life	978-0-87083-417-2
The Knowledge of Life	978-0-87083-419-6
The Tree of Life	978-0-87083-300-7
The Economy of God	978-0-87083-415-8
The Divine Economy	978-0-87083-268-0
God's New Testament Economy	978-0-87083-199-7
The World Situation and God's Move	978-0-87083-092-1
Christ vs. Religion	978-0-87083-010-5
The All-inclusive Christ	978-0-87083-020-4
Gospel Outlines	978-0-87083-039-6
Character	978-0-87083-322-9
The Secret of Experiencing Christ	978-0-87083-227-7
The Life and Way for the Practice of the Church Life	978-0-87083-785-2
The Basic Revelation in the Holy Scriptures	978-0-87083-105-8
The Crucial Revelation of Life in the Scriptures	978-0-87083-372-4
The Spirit with Our Spirit	978-0-87083-798-2
Christ as the Reality	978-0-87083-047-1
The Central Line of the Divine Revelation	978-0-87083-960-3
The Full Knowledge of the Word of God	978-0-87083-289-5
Watchman Nee—A Seer of the Divine Revelation ...	978-0-87083-625-1

Titles by Watchman Nee:

How to Study the Bible	978-0-7363-0407-8
God's Overcomers	978-0-7363-0433-7
The New Covenant	978-0-7363-0088-9
The Spiritual Man • 3 volumes	978-0-7363-0269-2
Authority and Submission	978-0-7363-0185-5
The Overcoming Life	978-1-57593-817-2
The Glorious Church	978-0-87083-745-6
The Prayer Ministry of the Church	978-0-87083-860-6
The Breaking of the Outer Man and the Release ...	978-1-57593-955-1
The Mystery of Christ	978-1-57593-954-4
The God of Abraham, Isaac, and Jacob	978-0-87083-932-0
The Song of Songs	978-0-87083-872-9
The Gospel of God • 2 volumes	978-1-57593-953-7
The Normal Christian Church Life	978-0-87083-027-3
The Character of the Lord's Worker	978-1-57593-322-1
The Normal Christian Faith	978-0-87083-748-7
Watchman Nee's Testimony	978-0-87083-051-8

Available at
Christian bookstores, or contact Living Stream Ministry
2431 W. La Palma Ave. • Anaheim, CA 92801
1-800-549-5164 • www.livingstream.com